Shh!
We're writing the
Constitution

BY JEAN FRITZ

PICTURES BY TOMIE dePAOLA
COVER ILLUSTRATION BY DAVID SMALL

PUFFIN BOOKS
AN IMPRINT OF PENGUIN GROUP (USA)

My thanks to James H. Hutson of the Library of Congress
for his generous and critical assistance.

PUFFIN BOOKS

Published by the Penguin Group

Penguin Group (USA) LLC

375 Hudson Street

New York, New York 10014

USA * Canada * UK * Ireland * Australia
New Zealand * India * South Africa * China

penguin.com

A Penguin Random House Company

First published in the United States of America by G. P. Putnam's Sons,
a division of Penguin Putnam Books for Young Readers, 1987
Published by PaperStar, a division of Penguin Putnam Books for Young Readers, 1998
Published by Puffin Books, a division of Penguin Young Readers Group, 2009
Reissued by Puffin Books, an imprint of Penguin Young Readers Group, 2015

THE LIBRARY OF CONGRESS HAS CATALOGED THE G. P. PUTNAM'S SONS EDITION AS FOLLOWS:

Fritz, Jean. Shhh! We're Writing the Constitution.

"The Constitution of the United States": p.

Bibliography: p. Summary: Describes how the Constitution came to be written and ratified. Also
includes the full text of the document produced by the Constitutional Convention of 1787.

ISBN 0-399-21403-8 (hardcover)

1. United States Constitutional Convention (1787)—Juvenile literature.

2. United States—Constitutional history—Juvenile literature.

[1. United States. Constitutional Convention (1787). 2. United States—Constitutional history.

3. United States—Constitution.]

I. dePaola, Tomie, ill. II. Title.

KF4520.Z9F75 1987 342.73'029 86-30229 347

Puffin Books ISBN 978-0-698-11624-5

Manufactured in China

14 16 18 20 19 17 15 13

To
Daniel Fritz
and
Michael Scott Fritz

DON'T TREAD ON ME

After the Revolutionary War most people in America were glad that they were no longer British. Still, they were not ready to call themselves Americans. The last thing they wanted was to become a nation. They were citizens of their own separate states, just as they had always been: each state different, each state proud of its own character, each state quick to poke fun at other states. To Southerners, New Englanders might be "no-account Yankees." To New Englanders, Pennsylvanians might be "lousy Buckskins." But to everyone the states themselves were all important. "Sovereign states," they called them. They loved the sound of "sovereign" because it meant that they were their own bosses.

George Washington, however, scoffed at the idea of "sovereign states." He knew that the states could not be truly independent for long and survive. Ever since the Declaration of Independence had been signed, people had referred to the country as the United States of America. It was about time, he thought, for them to act and feel united.

7

Once during the war Washington had decided it would be a good idea if his troops swore allegiance to the United States. As a start, he lined up some troops from New Jersey and asked them to take such an oath. They looked at Washington as if he'd taken leave of his senses. How could they do that? they cried. New Jersey was their country!

So Washington dropped the idea. In time, he hoped, the states would see that they needed to become one nation, united under a strong central government.

But that time would be long in coming. For now, as they started out on their independence, the thirteen states were satisfied to be what they called a federation, a kind of voluntary league of states. In other words, each state legislature sent delegates to a Continental Congress which was supposed to act on matters of common concern.

In September 1774, when the First Continental Congress met, the common concern was Great Britain. Two years later, after the Declaration of Independence had been signed, the concern was that the country needed some kind of government. Not a fully developed government because of course they had their states. All they wanted were some basic rules to hold them together to do whatever needed to be done. So the Congress wrote the Articles of Confederation which outlined rules for a "firm league of friendship." In practice, however, the states did not always feel a firm need to follow any rules.

The Congress, for instance, could ask the states to contribute money to pay the country's debts, but if the states didn't feel like contributing, no one could make them. Congress could declare war but it couldn't fight unless the states felt like supplying soldiers. The trouble was that their president had no definite powers and the country had no overall legal system. So although the Congress could make all the rules it wanted, it couldn't enforce any of them. Much of the time the states didn't even bother to send delegates to the meetings.

By 1786, it was becoming obvious that changes were needed. People were in debt, a few states were printing paper money that was all but worthless, and in the midst of this disorder some people could see that America would fall apart if it didn't have a sound central government with power to act for all the states. George Washington, of course, was one who had felt strongly about this for a long time. Alexander Hamilton was another. Born and brought up in the Caribbean Islands, he had no patience with the idea of state loyalty. America was nothing but a monster with thirteen heads, he said. James Madison from Virginia wanted a strong America too. He was a little man, described as being "no bigger than half a piece of soap," but he had big ideas for his country.

In 1786 these men, among others, suggested to the Congress that all the states send delegates to a Grand Convention in Philadelphia to improve the existing form of government. It sounded innocent. Just a matter of revising the old Articles of Confederation to make the government work better. No one would quarrel with that.

But they did.

Rhode Island refused to have anything to do with the convention. Patrick Henry, when asked to be a delegate from Virginia, said he "smelt a rat" and wouldn't go. Willie Jones of North Carolina didn't say what he smelled, but he wouldn't go either.

But in the end the convention was scheduled to meet in the State House in Philadelphia on May 14, 1787.

James (or "Jemmy") Madison was so worked up about it that he arrived from Virginia eleven days early. George Washington left his home, Mount Vernon, on May 9 with a headache and an upset stomach, but he arrived in Philadelphia on the night of May 13th. The next morning a few delegates from Pennsylvania and a few from Virginia came to the meeting but there needed to be seven states present to conduct business. Since there were only two, the meeting was adjourned.

It was May 25th before delegates from enough states showed up. They blamed their delays on the weather, muddy roads, personal business, lack of money. Delegates from New Hampshire couldn't scrape up enough money to come until late July, but even so, they beat John Francis Mercer of Maryland. He sauntered into the State House on August 6th.

The most colorful arrival was that of Benjamin Franklin who at eighty-one was the oldest of the delegates. Because he experienced so much pain when he was bounced about in a carriage, Franklin came to the convention in a Chinese sedan chair carried by four prisoners from the Philadelphia jail. (He lived in the city so they didn't have far to carry him.)

In all, there would be fifty-five delegates, although coming and going as they did, there were seldom more than thirty there at the same time. The first thing the delegates did was to elect George Washington president of the convention. They escorted him to his official chair on a raised platform. Then the other members of the convention took their seats at tables draped with green woolen cloth. James Madison sat in the front of the room and as soon as the talking began, he began writing. Never absent for a single day, he kept a record of all that was said during the next four months, stopping only when he, himself, wanted to speak.

They knew that there would be many arguments in this room, but they agreed that they didn't want the whole country listening in and taking sides. They would keep the proceedings a secret. So before every meeting the door was locked. Sentries were stationed in the hall. And even though it turned out to be a hot summer, the windows were kept closed. Why should they risk eavesdroppers? Members were not supposed to write gossipy letters home. Nor to answer nosy questions. Nor to discuss their business with outsiders. Benjamin Franklin was the one who had to be watched. He meant no harm but he did love to talk, especially at parties, so if he seemed about to spill the beans, another delegate was ready to leap into the conversation and change the subject.

For fifty-five men to keep a secret for four months was an accomplishment in itself. But they did. Of course this didn't prevent rumors from starting. Once it was rumored that the convention was planning to invite the second son of George the Third to become King of America. The delegates were furious. They might not be able to say what they were going to do, but they had no trouble saying what they were *not* going to do. And they were not inviting the second or third son of George the Third or of anyone else to be King of America.

If the people of the country were afraid of what might happen in the convention, so were the delegates themselves. They didn't call the document they were working on a "constitution"; they referred to it as "the plan." Because they knew that the country was sensitive to the word "national," they tried to stick to "federal," a word they were used to and one which didn't reduce the power of the states. But after Edmund Randolph, Governor of Virginia, had presented what came to be called the Virginia Plan, he spoke right out.

In the Virginia Plan, Randolph explained, there would be three branches of government. The executive branch would have a head who would be responsible for running the government. The legislative branch would be made up of two houses which would make laws. The House of Representatives would be elected directly by the people; the Senate, the smaller and supposedly more coolheaded body, would be elected by the House. Together they would be called the Congress. The third branch would be the judiciary headed by a Supreme Court, which would make sure that laws were constitutional and were properly obeyed.

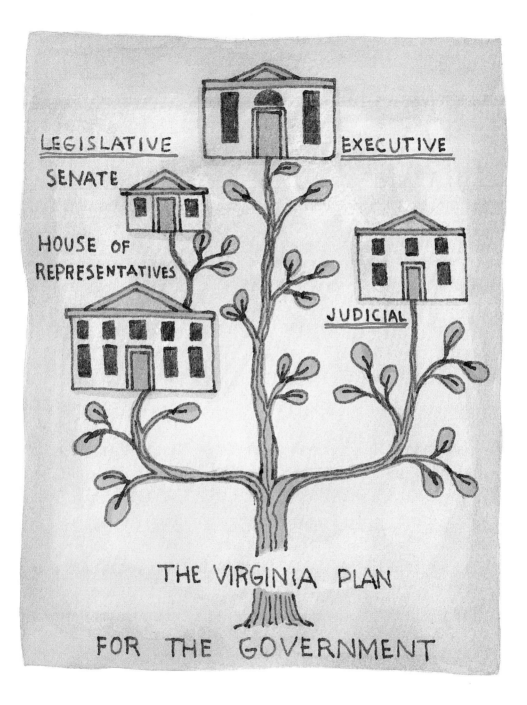

Edmund Randolph was a tall, handsome, likable man and nothing he said at first seemed alarming. Some of the states had constitutions that were similar to the one he described. Besides, the members knew that after Randolph's plan had been discussed, other members would have a chance to present their plans. But at the end of his speech Randolph did arouse his audience. It should be clear, he said, that his resolutions were not merely for a federal government but for a national government that would be supreme over the states.

There was a dead silence.

Pierce Butler of South Carolina was one of the first to recover. He jumped down hard on the word "national" but John Dickinson of Delaware said there was nothing wrong with the word. "We *are* a nation!" he declared.

No! For Elbridge Gerry of Massachusetts this kind of talk was scary. He was a thin, worrying sort of man who was sometimes called "Grumbletonian" behind his back. National? he sputtered. How could they think national? They had been sent here to revise the Articles of Confederation, not to destroy them.

17

As the meetings went on, all kinds of fear surfaced. The smaller states with fewer people were afraid of the larger states which had more people. In the past the votes of all states, no matter what their population, had counted the same. But a national government would be more concerned with individual people than with the states themselves. So what would happen to the small states now? And what kind of government were they forming? Some people were afraid of a "high-toned" or aristocratic government run by a small, privileged, wealthy group, the way a monarchy was usually run. Others were just as afraid of the common people having too much power. They weren't capable of governing, it was said.

Eventually the convention did agree on a national legislature to consist of two houses but before final acceptance, the word "national" was crossed out.

Still, there were so many questions to decide. What about the person who was to be the executive or head of the government? Should there be just one person? If so, would he seem like a king? Why not three people, each representing a different part of the country? But what if they fought among themselves? What if they couldn't reach an agreement? Should the executive be paid a salary? (Yes, said Madison. Don't count on patriotism.) But who should pay the salary—the states or the government of the United States? How should the executive be chosen? By the people? By the states? By a branch of the United States legislature? By electors? By lot? (They had to vote sixty times before they could settle this question.) And

how long should the executive serve? If he were thought to be guilty of misconduct, could they impeach him? Could they remove him from office?

Alexander Hamilton was one of the few who wanted the president to serve a long term, perhaps even for life. He thought it would be embarrassing to watch a lot of ex-presidents wandering around like ghosts. But suppose you had a long-term president, Franklin pointed out. And suppose he turned out to be a bad president. What then? Out of simple kindness they ought to provide some way to get rid of him. Otherwise, Franklin chuckled, the only thing they could do would be to shoot him.

In the end it was decided that there should be a single executive who would be paid out of the Treasury of the new government. He would be chosen by electors from each state, and he would serve four years. And yes, if it was necessary, he could be impeached.

But what if he should die while in office? Or be impeached? Who would take his place? So there had to be a vice president, the one who came in second in the presidential election. And since the vice president should do more than just wait around to see if the president would make it through his term, he was given the job of presiding over the Senate.

Mr. Randolph finished presenting his plan on May 29 and for the next two weeks—until June 13—the convention went over it. Some measures were voted on, some would be revised, and all would be discussed again and again. But there was also the chance that the whole plan would be scrapped for something else. After a day's recess, on June 15, William Paterson of New Jersey stood up. Only five feet two, he wasn't as impressive a figure as Mr. Randolph, but he was a cheerful, modest, likable man. Still, he didn't approve of a single idea of Mr. Randolph's. The government should be a federation of states as it was now, with each state having an equal vote, he said. It should consist of one legislative body with several executives at its head. According to Mr. Paterson, the Virginia Plan was impractical, illegal, and expensive. How could so many members of Congress, he asked, find the money to travel from all over the country to attend meetings?

J. MADISON   W. PATERSON

When James Madison answered Mr. Paterson, it was as if he were fencing. Madison danced all around Mr. Paterson's arguments, thrusting at first one point, then another until it seemed as if there were nothing left of William Paterson's plan. And there wasn't. When the delegates were asked to vote in favor of one of the two plans, Mr. Randolph's won. Seven states against three. (Maryland's delegation was divided.) Randolph's plan still had to be thrashed out, but the idea of a federation was dead. With this vote the delegates committed themselves to write a constitution for a new nation, whether all of them were willing to call it that or not.

But so much work lay ahead! They would be at it all summer, the delegates said, and some sent for their families to join them. John Dickinson of Delaware spent much of his free time writing to his four-year-old daughter, Maria, whom he always addressed as "Pa's Precious." Rufus King of Massachusetts and Luther Martin of Maryland went to the library and took out books but never returned them. Sorry, they said, when asked about it; their servants must have failed to deliver them. Sorry or not, however, they had to pay for the books. Oliver

Ellsworth of Connecticut had the most interesting news to write home. He had shaken the hand of a woman who was two thousand years old, he said. An Egyptian mummy was on display in Philadelphia but Oliver wasn't content just to look. He wondered what the flesh was like, so he took out his knife and tested it. Like old smoked beef, he reported.

Meanwhile the people in Philadelphia did their best to keep the delegates happy. They entertained them, provided musicals, and so that they could work in peace and quiet, they covered the cobblestone street in front of the State House with gravel. Now carriages made less noise when they rolled past.

But there were some things Philadelphians couldn't change. The heat, for instance. It was a blistering summer, especially for the delegates from New England who, not used to such heat, sweated out the summer in woolen suits. And there were bluebottle flies. Philadelphia was bombarded by these huge, buzzing flies. They flung themselves at the windows of the State House, attacked delegates when they stepped outside,

and invaded bedrooms, buzzing all night in such a frenzy, they sounded insane.

Nor could Philadelphia do anything about the prison which stood in front of the State House yard. It was a four-story building and as soon as the delegates came into the yard, prisoners crowded against their windows and pushed long "begging" poles through the iron bars. Attached to the end of each pole was a cloth cap for collecting money. The prisoners would dangle the poles, wiggle them, and cry out to be noticed. And if

the delegates were not generous enough (and how could they be generous enough every day?), the prisoners would jeer and call the delegates nasty names.

It couldn't have been any fun to sit all day in a stuffy room, arguing, and then be insulted as soon as they stepped out for a breath of fresh air. On the other hand, the delegates may have had too much on their minds to pay attention.

Certainly they suffered in many ways and it was a wonder they didn't quit. Some did. Two delegates from New York who didn't like the way the convention was going went home. But most knew that they were deciding the future of their country, one which would be larger and different from anything they could imagine now. Sometimes when a delegate worried that "the people" wouldn't like this or "the people" wouldn't like that, James Madison became impatient. Who knew what the people would like? he asked. Their job was to make the best possible government, not simply please the people. And all the time George Washington sat in front of them, his expression stern as if he were saying, "Now or never." It would be hard to walk out on Washington.

Yet it was sometimes hard to stay. Especially when Luther Martin of Maryland took the floor. He was a tall, mussed-up looking man who loved the sound of his own voice so much that once he started talking, he couldn't bear to stop. He talked loudly and passionately. He repeated himself and indeed was so boring that Madison didn't bother to write it all down and Benjamin Franklin went to sleep.

But as the convention droned on and on, the delegates worried. Was it possible for them ever to agree on a constitution? The biggest stumbling block was the question of how power should be divided in the government. Should the states be represented in Congress according to the population of each state? Yes, said the large states with large populations. No, said the small states with small populations. Madison tried to point out that the large states would have no reason to gang up on the smaller states. The large states had so little in common, they would probably end up, he said, as rivals, not friends. But the small states were not convinced.

At one point the tension was so great that Franklin suggested they ask a minister to start them off every day with a prayer. But they couldn't even agree on this. A delegate from North Carolina pointed out that there wasn't enough money to pay a minister. Hamilton said that the appearance of a minister would start rumors. People would say that if the convention was suddenly in need of prayer, it must be in deep trouble.

In particular, the small states wanted to know if they would have an equal vote in the Senate. The delegates could not reach a decision. When they took a vote, it came out a tie. Five, yes; five, no, with Georgia's delegates divided. The small states became so bitter that once they threatened to break off from the rest of the country and make their own treaties with foreign nations. This was the lowest point of the whole summer. The convention was held together now, Luther Martin said, by "no more than the strength of a hair." Washington, not easily discouraged, admitted that he "almost despaired," and indeed his feelings must have shown on his face. He had his "Valley Forge look," people said.

Perhaps the weather helped to break the stalemate. The month-long heat wave broke over the weekend of July 14 and 15 and by Monday, July 16, the delegates seemed to recognize how urgent it was to find a way to agree. And they did. They called it the Great Compromise. Every state would have two members in the Senate (with equal votes) while the House of Representatives would have one representative for every forty thousand inhabitants. (Later this was changed to read "not to exceed one for every thirty Thousand.")

It was such a relief to have this settled that the convention appointed a committee of five to put their resolutions in order and make a document that would read like a constitution. Then the delegates voted themselves a ten day vacation from July 26 to August 6. George Washington went fishing and caught a mess of perch near Trenton. It was a welcome diversion; still, as always he was homesick for Mount Vernon. He had written home earlier that he wouldn't be back before harvest and "God knows how long it may be after." He wanted the honeysuckle against the house nailed up. "Have you thinned out the carrots?" he asked.

Six weeks of work still lay ahead after the convention reassembled. Throughout the discussions there had been trouble not only between the large states and the small states but between the northern states and the southern states. The southern states worried about their trade. Since the House of Representatives was dominated by northern states where more people lived, would it be fair to the south? The House had the power to tax what was sold and sent out of the states and to tax what was brought into the states. So what would happen to tobacco, rice, and indigo grown in the south and sold abroad? What would happen to slaves brought into the south? Would the north try to get rid of slavery altogether? Some northern delegates were quick to say that was exactly what they wanted, but some southern delegates were just as quick to say that they wouldn't belong to a government that dictated their private business.

It was clear that if they wanted a constitution, the north and south would have to strike a bargain. So the northern states agreed to continue the slave trade until 1808 and the southern states agreed to give up their demand that commercial regulations had to be passed by a two-thirds vote of both Houses. In addition, no one would have to pay more than ten dollars tax on a slave brought into the country.

And there were other questions. Where would the government be located? New York? Philadelphia? A special district should be set aside, they said, not more than ten miles square. But since they couldn't decide where it should be, they de-

GOUVERNEUR MORRIS

cided to let the new Congress take care of it.

How about letting foreigners be members of Congress? Gouverneur Morris (called "The Tall Boy" of the convention) pointed out that if it took seven years to learn how to be a shoemaker, a foreigner ought to spend fourteen years to learn how to be an American legislator. In the end a senator was required to be a citizen for nine years; a representative—seven years; and the chief executive, or president, had to be native born.

They made provisions for new states to join the Union and specified how additions or changes to the Constitution could be made in the future. These would be called amendments but under no circumstances were they to change the type of government the delegates had created. The delegates didn't want any American dukes or lords suddenly popping up in their society. "No Title of Nobility," they said, "shall be granted by the United States."

Now the end was actually in sight, but how should they present the Constitution to the states? Should each state legislature vote on whether it would accept (or ratify) the Constitution? No, they decided; the state legislators could not be trusted. They would want to keep their own power in their state and would vote no. It would be better if each state called its own special convention. Next came the question: How many states had to ratify the Constitution before it became the law of the land? Some delegates wanted all thirteen states to ratify but everyone knew Rhode Island wouldn't do it and New York was doubtful so it was agreed that if nine states ratified, they'd have a nation. Any that didn't ratify would simply not be in the Union.

On September 8 the Constitution was sent to a committee to write it up in final form. Four days later a revised and very elegant sounding Constitution was presented to the delegates. "We the People," it began. It was impressive but it was also scary. Some of the delegates didn't think of themselves as "We the People." It gave them a strange feeling to have created a nation that they didn't really know. All at once some had last minute thoughts. They had not included a Bill of Rights which spelled out the rights of individual persons, it was pointed out. There was no mention of freedom of religion, freedom of speech, trial by jury—all those rights which they'd cherished and which many states had listed in their state constitutions.

Madison sighed. There was no need for a Bill of Rights, he said. It was taken for granted that individuals kept all the rights that they didn't specifically give over to the government.

Finally, with some changes, the Constitution was sent out to be engrossed on parchment, an official document for the delegates to sign. When it came back the delegates looked at it in wonder. After all, this was the first time that a people had written down rules to start a nation off from scratch. On paper the Constitution looked so *real* that, Washington declared, it was "a little short of a miracle."

Still, it was not perfect, Benjamin Franklin pointed out. He disagreed with some parts but then he wasn't perfect either. None of them were and he was convinced that this was the best that they could do. He hoped the delegates would give their new Constitution a chance. Let them not undo their summer's

work, he begged, by carrying their old arguments into the public. Let them stand together.

Some members, like Luther Martin who would not have signed, had already gone home. But there were forty-two delegates present on September 17 and thirty-nine signed. At the last minute three backed out. Elbridge Gerry was one. Without a Bill of Rights, he said, he couldn't put his name down. Edmund Randolph (whose Virginia Plan had actually formed the basis of the Constitution) got cold feet. Perhaps he'd been too hasty. Perhaps he was still too much of a Virginian to be an American too. Perhaps he should wait to see how the country reacted before he made up his mind. George Mason, also of Virginia, refused to sign.

Now it was up to the country. After so much secrecy, people didn't know what to expect, but once they had read the Consti-

tution, they were quick to take sides. Those who were for it called themselves Federalists. Those against were called Anti-Federalists although the "antis" said they were the true Federalists and those in favor of the Constitution should be called Nationalists.

It took more than six months for the states, one by one, to call their conventions, debate, and vote. Meanwhile Alexander Hamilton, James Madison, and another strong Federalist, John Jay, began writing newspaper articles explaining just how the new Constitution would work.

They showed how the different branches of government would serve as a check on each other so that no one branch or no one person could become too powerful. Steeped in history, these men understood human nature and the temptations of

power. They might not expect to make a government absolutely safe from all forms of tyranny, but their object was to create a kind of obstacle game which would keep the government in balance. Indeed, they talked so much of checks and balances that this might describe the kind of game it was. Every bill the House of Representatives passed, for instance, had to go to the Senate for its approval. If it made it through the Senate, then it had to go to the president for his signature. If he did not like the bill, he could veto or refuse to sign it. But the House and the Senate still had another chance. If two-thirds of their members voted for it, then it would pass anyway. A final Big Check lay in the Supreme Court which could in the course of legal proceedings decide if a law (even a state law) was constitutional or not.

There was a whole network of such checks. Although the president could appoint ambassadors to other countries, judges to the Supreme Court, and a variety of other officers, the Senate had to approve his choices. Any amendment proposed to the Constitution had to be submitted to the states for their approval. Now how, the Federalists asked, could tyranny slip through such a well-ordered system? Besides, the people themselves had the controlling power. Every four years they would be electing their president and at stated intervals they would also be electing their representatives to Congress. The arguments of the Federalists were so strong and so well written that many people gradually grew used to the idea of becoming a nation.

But not all. Patrick Henry took one look at the first words of the Constitution and saw red. "We the people!" he snorted. Since when had they become a single people? He'd known something hadn't smelled right and here was this fancy document that with a single stroke wiped out their thirteen separate identities. Besides, it didn't say one word about those basic rights that they had fought a war over.

All over the country people argued about a Bill of Rights. In Connecticut Noah Webster, educator and compiler of dictionaries, contended that such a bill would be nonsense. How could you list all the rights a person had? he asked. Would you include the right to go fishing in good weather? The right of people to turn over in bed at night?

But most people were serious about the issue and many were

unhappy. Federalists tried to reassure them. Once the government was formed, they pointed out, the Constitution could easily be amended to include those rights that they wanted. All they had to do was to recommend improvements and then go ahead and ratify. If they didn't, they'd end up with neither a government nor a Bill of Rights.

Delaware started off the state conventions and on December 7 was the first to ratify the Constitution. Its vote was unanimous as was New Jersey's on December 18 and Georgia's on January 2, 1788.

Other states had a harder time reaching an agreement. Pennsylvania ratified on December 12 with a vote of 46–23; Connecticut on January 9 with a vote of 128–40. Massachusetts argued for a month and although it finally ratified on February 6, the vote was close: 187 to 168. Maryland came along on April 28 (63–11) and South Carolina on May 23 (149–73).

On June 21 New Hampshire was the ninth state to ratify the Constitution (57–47). And with its vote the United States of America officially became a nation.

But people were still anxious for the big states to join so that the new nation would seem more impressive. Virginia was an important state, but if Patrick Henry had had his way, it would never have joined. He spoke against the Constitution for two weeks, once giving eight speeches in one day, once speaking all day long. But on June 26 the Virginia convention did ratify (89–79). A month later on July 26, New York, which had never been enthusiastic, also voted yes (30–27).

North Carolina, however, voted no and Rhode Island didn't even bother to hold a convention. When they saw the results of the other elections, they accused the rest of the country of seceding from *them*. Eventually they changed their minds. North Carolina joined the Union in November 1789, and Rhode Island in May 1790.

But Philadelphia couldn't wait for all the states to come into the Union before celebrating. As soon as Virginia had ratified, Philadelphia got ready for a big Fourth of July celebration. Indeed, the Grand Procession that marched through the city from eight in the morning until six in the evening was so grand, it was a wonder that there were enough people left over to watch. Leading the parade was a herald with a trumpet proclaiming the New Age. Riders on horseback carried banners that celebrated everything and every person worth celebrating. A float made to look like a giant blue eagle rolled up the cobblestone streets, followed by an enormous framed Constitution propped up in a carriage pulled by six white horses. A

fancy building with thirteen columns representing the new nation was pulled in a vehicle drawn by ten white horses. Of course there was music. High-stepping bands, beating and blowing, kept the town tapping to their tunes.

And people! Four hundred and fifty architects and carpenters marched in the procession. There were sawmakers and filecutters, farmers with their four-ox plows, weavers, tailors, goldsmiths, gunsmiths, brickmakers, clockmakers, boat builders, coopers, bakers, corsetmakers, and preachers. The Federal ship *Union* mounted with twenty guns brought up the rear of the procession. And everyone ended up at a picnic spread out for seventeen thousand people.

The country may have kicked and screamed its way into becoming a nation, but once there it celebrated. Bells pealed and cannon roared as state after state acknowledged that the Constitution they had adopted was now "the Supreme Law of the Land."

Two of America's most important statesmen, however, were not in the country during any of the Constitutional proceedings. John Adams, who would be our second president, was in England, serving as our ambassador. Thomas Jefferson, who would be our third president, was our ambassador to France. When John Adams, just arriving in Boston in 1788, heard the news that the Constitution had been adopted, he wrote to Jefferson.

"As we say at sea," he wrote, "huzza for the new world and farewell to the old one!"

And Thomas Jefferson, once he felt satisfied that a Bill of Rights would be included, called the new Constitution "unquestionably the wisest ever yet presented to men."

Notes

Page 8. The thirteen states were New Hampshire, Massachusetts, Connecticut, Rhode Island, New York, New Jersey, Pennsylvania, Delaware, Maryland, Virginia, North Carolina, South Carolina, and Georgia.

Page 9. The Articles of Confederation were adopted by the Continental Congress on November 15, 1777. Article One established that the name the *United States of America* be given to the union of the colonies. Article Two guaranteed that each state would retain its own sovereignty. The Constitutional Convention was held in what is now known as Independence Hall in Philadelphia.

Page 10. The idea for a Grand Convention was proposed in September 1786 at a meeting (the Annapolis Convention) called by Virginia to work out disputes over states' rights to navigation and trade on the Potomac River. It became obvious that a general system of interstate commerce needed to be worked out and it was with this excuse that the Grand Convention was suggested.

It was also obvious that the states were not managing well on their own. During the Annapolis Convention farmers in western Massachusetts, angry that their farms were being taken from them to pay their debts, staged a rebellion. Led by a former army captain, Daniel Shays, rebel bands forced courts to close and eventually marched, twelve-hundred strong, to Springfield, Massachusetts, with the intention of taking the government arsenal located there. Although Massachusetts was able to put down the rebellion, the entire country was alarmed by the violence and realized how weak the Articles of Confederation really were.

Patrick Henry was the orator who gave the famous "Liberty or

Death" speech before the Revolution. Willie (pronounced Wylie) Jones had been a member of the Continental Congress and was prominent in North Carolina political affairs.

Page 11.   Franklin had brought the chair with him from France. He suffered from gout and stones in the bladder.

Page 14.   "National" referred to a central government that had power over and above that of the states. "Federal" implied a government formed by an association of states which gave up none of their powers and joined to promote measures that would be mutually helpful.

In 1913 the Seventeenth Amendment provided that senators should be elected directly by the people.

Page 18.   The word "national" is never used in the Constitution.

Twenty-one different days were spent discussing the presidency, but the final decisions did not come until late in the convention.

In discussing the chief executive and officers of the government, the Constitution always refers to them as "men." Women did not even have the right to vote at that time nor did they achieve this right until 1920 when the Nineteenth Amendment was passed.

Page 20.   The delegates at the Constitutional Convention had no idea that political parties would develop in the nation and that it would be awkward if the president and the vice president came from different parties. The Twelfth Amendment, in 1804, provided for separate elections for the two offices.

There was disagreement at first about what the president should be officially called. When Washington was elected president, John Adams, the new vice president, insisted that the president should be called "His Most Benign Highness" or at least "His Highness." If he were just "Mr. President," Adams said, how would anyone know he wasn't just a president of a fire company? But in spite of John Adams, the president has always been simply "Mr. President."

Page 28. Votes were counted by states. Each state had one vote and at this particular meeting only eleven states were present.

Page 29. The winter that the Continental Army spent in Valley Forge during the war was, of course, the low point of the war and the low point for Washington.

Part of the Compromise included the provision that the House of Representatives alone would have the right to originate money bills that had to do with raising revenues. The Senate could accept, reject, or alter such bills.

Page 31. There was argument as to how slaves should be counted in a state's population. If slaves were counted as individuals, the slave states would, of course, have a far higher representation in Congress than if they were not counted at all. In the end it was decided that five slaves would be counted the same as three free white men.

The underlying and deep division in the country about slavery was evident even at the time of the writing of the Declaration of Independence. It became an ever more burning issue as time went on and eventually erupted in the Civil War. The Thirteenth, Fourteenth, and Fifteenth amendments abolished slavery and guaranteed civil rights and voting rights to United States citizens, including former slaves.

The district established (1790–1791) by Congress for the capital had been selected by George Washington and was called the District of Columbia. It is more commonly referred to today as Washington, D.C.

Page 32. Gouverneur Morris gave 173 speeches during the convention, more than any other delegate. Madison gave 161, but Jared Ingersoll of Pennsylvania did not open his mouth once during the meetings.

Page 34. As Franklin was about to sign the Constitution, he said that all summer he had been studying the design painted at the top of George Washington's chair. It was a picture of the sun with rays emanating from it, but Franklin couldn't tell whether it was a rising sun or a setting sun. Now he knew. It was a rising sun, he said.

Page 35.   Some people who knew Edmund Randolph well were not surprised when he suddenly changed his mind about signing. He was a wavering sort of man, they said.

Page 36.   When Washington became president in 1789, he appointed John Jay the first Chief Justice of the Supreme Court.

The newspaper articles written by Hamilton, Madison, and Jay turned out to be a collection of eighty-five essays. Later they were put in book form and became famous as *The Federalist Papers.*

Page 40.   The first ten amendments, known as the Bill of Rights, were ratified in 1791.

The Constitution of the United States[*]

We the People of the United States, in Order to form a more perfect Union, establish Justice, insure domestic Tranquillity, provide for the common defence, promote the general Welfare, and secure the Blessings of Liberty to ourselves and our Posterity, do ordain and establish this Constitution for the United States of America.

ARTICLE I

Section 1. All legislative Powers herein granted shall be vested in a Congress of the United States, which shall consist of a Senate and a House of Representatives.

Section 2. The House of Representatives shall be composed of Members chosen every second Year by the People of the several States, and the Electors in each State shall have [the] Qualifications requisite for Electors of the most numerous Branch of the State Legislature.

No Person shall be a Representative who shall not have attained to the Age of twenty five Years, and been seven Years a Citizen of the United States, and who shall not, when elected, be an Inhabitant of that State in which he shall be chosen.

Representatives and direct Taxes shall be apportioned among the several States which may be included within this Union, according to their respective Numbers, which shall be determined by adding to the whole Number of free Persons, including those bound to Service for a Term of Years, and excluding Indians not taxed, three fifths of all other Persons. The actual Enumeration shall be made within three Years

---

[*] After the engrossed parchment sent by the Federal Convention to Congress on September 18, 1787. Reproduced in *The Records of the Federal Convention*, Max Farrand, ed., vol. II, pp. 651–666.

after the first Meeting of the Congress of the United States, and within every subsequent Term of ten Years, in such Manner as they shall by Law direct. The Number of Representatives shall not exceed one for every thirty Thousand, but each State shall have at Least one Representative; and until such enumeration shall be made, the State of New Hampshire shall be entitled to chuse three, Massachusetts eight, Rhode-Island and Providence Plantations one, Connecticut five, New-York six, New Jersey four, Pennsylvania eight, Delaware one, Maryland six, Virginia ten, North Carolina five, South Carolina five, and Georgia three.

When vacancies happen in the Representation from any State, the Executive Authority thereof shall issue Writs of Election to fill such Vacancies.

The House of Representatives shall chuse their Speaker and other Officers; and shall have the sole Power of Impeachment.

Section 3. The Senate of the United States shall be composed of two Senators from each State, chosen by the Legislature thereof, for six Years; and each Senator shall have one Vote.

Immediately after they shall be assembled in Consequence of the first Election, they shall be divided as equally as may be into three Classes. The Seats of the Senators of the first Class shall be vacated at the Expiration of the second Year, and of the second Class at the Expiration of the fourth Year, and of the third Class at the Expiration of the sixth Year, so that one third may be chosen every second Year; and if Vacancies happen by Resignation, or otherwise, during the Recess of the Legislature of any State, the Executive thereof may make temporary Appointments until the next Meeting of the Legislature, which shall then fill such Vacancies.

No person shall be a Senator who shall not have attained to the Age of thirty Years, and been nine Years a Citizen of the United States, and who shall not, when elected, be an Inhabitant of that State for which he shall be chosen.

The Vice President of the United States shall be President of the

Senate, but shall have no Vote, unless they be equally divided.

The Senate shall chuse their other Officers, and also a President pro tempore, in the Absence of the Vice President, or when he shall exercise the Office of President of the United States.

The Senate shall have the sole Power to try all Impeachments. When sitting for that Purpose, they shall be on Oath or Affirmation. When the President of the United States [is tried,] the Chief Justice shall preside: And no Person shall be convicted without the Concurrence of two thirds of the Members present.

Judgment in Cases of Impeachment shall not extend further than to removal from Office, and disqualification to hold and enjoy any Office of honor, Trust or Profit under the United States: but the Party convicted shall nevertheless be liable and subject to Indictment, Trial, Judgment and Punishment, according to Law.

Section 4. The Times, Places and Manner of holding Elections for Senators and Representatives shall be prescribed in each State by the Legislature thereof; but the Congress may at any time by Law make or alter such Regulations, except as to the Places of chusing Senators.

The Congress shall assemble at least once in every Year, and such Meeting shall be on the first Monday in December, unless they shall by Law appoint a different Day.

Section 5. Each House shall be the Judge of the Elections, Returns and Qualifications of its own Members, and a Majority of each shall constitute a Quorum to do Business; but a smaller Number may adjourn from day to day, and may be authorized to compel the Attendance of absent Members, in such Manner, and under such Penalties, as each House may provide.

Each House may determine the Rules of its Proceedings, punish its Members for disorderly Behaviour, and, with the Concurrence of two thirds, expel a Member.

Each House shall keep a Journal of its Proceedings, and from time to time publish the same, excepting such Parts as may in their Judgment

require Secrecy; and the Yeas and Nays of the Members of either House on any question shall, at the Desire of one fifth of those Present, be entered on the Journal.

Neither House, during the Session of Congress, shall, without the Consent of the other, adjourn for more than three days, nor to any other Place than that in which the two Houses shall be sitting.

Section 6. The Senators and Representatives shall receive a Compensation for their Services, to be ascertained by Law and paid out of the Treasury of the United States. They shall in all Cases except Treason, Felony and Breach of the Peace, be privileged from Arrest during their Attendance at the Session of their respective Houses, and in going to and returning from the same; and for any Speech or Debate in either House, they shall not be questioned in any other Place.

No Senator or Representative shall, during the Time for which he was elected, be appointed to any civil Office under the Authority of the United States which shall have been created, or the Emoluments whereof shall have been encreased during such time; and no Person holding any Office under the United States, shall be a Member of either House during his Continuance in Office.

Section 7. All Bills for raising Revenue shall originate in the House of Representatives; but the Senate may propose or concur with Amendments as on other Bills.

Every Bill which shall have passed the House of Representatives and the Senate, shall, before it become a Law, be presented to the President of the United States; if he approve he shall sign it, but if not he shall return it, with his Objections to that House in which it shall have originated, who shall enter the Objections at large on their Journal, and proceed to reconsider it. If after such Reconsideration two thirds of that House shall agree to pass the Bill, it shall be sent, together with the Objections, to the other House, by which it shall likewise be reconsidered, and, if approved by two thirds of that House, it shall become a Law. But in all such Cases the Votes of both Houses shall be determined by yeas and Nays, and the Names of the Persons voting for and against the Bill shall be entered on the Journal of each House respectively. If any Bill shall not be returned by the President within ten Days (Sundays excepted) after it shall have been presented to him, the Same shall be a Law, in like Manner as if he had signed it, unless the Congress by their Adjournment prevent its Return, in which Case it shall not be a Law.

Every Order, Resolution, or Vote to which the Concurrence of the Senate and House of Representatives may be necessary (except on a question of Adjournment) shall be presented to the President of the United States; and before the Same shall take Effect, shall be approved by him, or being disapproved by him, shall be repassed by two thirds of the Senate and House of Representatives, according to the Rules and Limitations prescribed in the Case of a Bill.

Section 8. The Congress shall have Power To lay and collect Taxes, Duties, Imposts and Excises, to pay the Debts and provide for the common Defence and general Welfare of the United States; but all Duties, Imposts and Excises shall be uniform throughout the United States;

To borrow Money on the credit of the United States;

To regulate Commerce with foreign Nations, and among the several States, and with the Indian Tribes;

To establish an uniform Rule of Naturalization, and uniform Laws on the subject of Bankruptcies throughout the United States;

To coin Money, regulate the Value thereof, and of foreign Coin, and fix the Standard of Weights and Measures;

To provide for the Punishment of counterfeiting the Securities and current Coin of the United States;

To establish Post Offices and post Roads;

To promote the Progress of Science and useful Arts, by securing for limited Times to Authors and Inventors the exclusive Right to their respective Writings and Discoveries;

To constitute Tribunals inferior to the supreme Court;

To define and punish Piracies and Felonies committed on the high seas, and Offences against the Law of Nations;

To declare War, grant Letters of Marque and Reprisal, and make Rules concerning Captures on Land and Water;

To raise and support Armies, but no Appropriation of Money to that Use shall be for a longer Term than two Years;

To provide and maintain a Navy;

To make Rules for the Government and Regulation of the land and naval Forces;

To provide for calling forth the Militia to execute the Laws of the Union, suppress Insurrections and repel Invasions;

To provide for organizing, arming, and disciplining the Militia, and for governing such Part of them as may be employed in the Service of the United States, reserving to the States respectively, the Appointment of the Officers, and the Authority of training the Militia according to the discipline prescribed by Congress;

To exercise exclusive Legislation in all Cases whatsoever, over such District (not exceeding ten Miles square) as may, by Cession of Particular States, and the Acceptance of Congress, become the Seat of Government of the United States, and to exercise like Authority over all Places purchased by the Consent of the Legislature of the State in which the Same shall be, for the Erection of Forts, Magazines, Arsenals, dock-Yards, and other needful Buildings;—And

To make all Laws which shall be necessary and proper for carrying into Execution the foregoing Powers, and all other Powers vested by this Constitution in the Government of the United States, or in any Department or Officer thereof.

Section 9. The Migration or Importation of such Persons as any of the States now existing shall think proper to admit, shall not be prohibited by the Congress prior to the Year one thousand eight hundred and eight, but a Tax or duty may be imposed on such Importation, not exceeding ten dollars for each Person.

The Privilege of the Writ of Habeas Corpus shall not be suspended, unless when in Cases of Rebellion or Invasion the public Safety may require it.

No Bill of Attainder or ex post facto Law shall be passed.

No Capitation, or other direct, Tax shall be laid, unless in Proportion to the Census or Enumeration herein before directed to be taken.

No Tax or Duty shall be laid on Articles exported from any State.

No Preference shall be given by any Regulation of Commerce or Revenue to the Ports of one State over those of another: nor shall Vessels bound to, or from, one State, be obliged to enter, clear, or pay Duties in another.

No Money shall be drawn from the Treasury, but in Consequence of Appropriations made by Law; and a regular Statement and Account of the Receipts and Expenditures of all public Money shall be published from time to time.

No Title of Nobility shall be granted by the United States: And no Person holding any Office of Profit or Trust under them shall, without the Consent of the Congress, accept of any present, Emolument, Office, or Title, of any kind whatever, from any King, Prince, or foreign State.

Section 10. No State shall enter into any Treaty, Alliance, or Confederation; grant Letters of Marque and Reprisal; coin Money; emit Bills of Credit; make any Thing but gold and silver Coin a Tender in Payment of Debts; pass any Bill of Attainder, ex post facto Law, or Law impairing the Obligation of Contracts, or grant any Title of Nobility.

No State shall, without the consent of [the] Congress, lay any Imposts or Duties on Imports or Exports, except what may be absolutely necessary for executing its inspection Laws: and the net Produce of all Duties and Imposts, laid by any State on Imports or Exports, shall be for the Use of the Treasury of the United States; and all such Laws shall be subject to the Revision and Controul of [the] Congress.

No State shall, without the Consent of Congress, lay any Duty of Tonnage, keep Troops, or Ships of War in time of Peace, enter into any Agreement or Compact with another State, or with a foreign Power, or engage in War, unless actually invaded, or in such imminent Danger as will not admit of delay.

Section 1. The executive Power shall be vested in a President of the United States of America. He shall hold his Office during the Term of four Years, and together with the Vice President, chosen for the same Term, be elected as follows

Each State shall appoint, in such Manner as the Legislature thereof may direct, a Number of Electors, equal to the whole Number of Senators and Representatives to which the State may be entitled in the Congress: but no Senator or Representative, or Person holding an Office of Trust or Profit under the United States, shall be appointed an Elector.

The Electors shall meet in their respective States, and vote by Ballot for two Persons, of whom one at least shall not be an Inhabitant of the same State with themselves. And they shall make a List of all the Persons voted for, and of the Number of Votes for each; which List they shall sign and certify, and transmit sealed to the Seat of Government of the United States, directed to the President of the Senate. The President of the Senate shall, in the Presence of the Senate and House of Representatives, open all the Certificates, and the Votes shall then be counted. The Person having the greatest Number of Votes shall be the President, if such Number be a Majority of the whole Number of Electors appointed; and if there be more than one who have such Majority, and have an equal Number of Votes, then the House of Representatives shall immediately chuse by Ballot one of them for President; and if no Person have a Majority, then from the five highest on the List the said House shall in like Manner chuse the President. But in chusing the President the Votes shall be taken by States, the Representation from each State having one Vote; A quorum for this Purpose shall consist of a Member or Members from two thirds of the States, and a Majority of all the States shall be necessary to a Choice. In every Case, after the Choice of the President, the Person having the greatest Number of Votes of the Electors shall be the Vice President. But if there should remain two or more who have equal Votes, the Senate shall chuse from them by Ballot the Vice President.

The Congress may determine the Time of chusing the Electors, and the Day on which they shall give their Votes; which Day shall be the same throughout the United States.

No person except a natural born Citizen, or a Citizen of the United States, at the time of the Adoption of this Constitution, shall be eligible to the Office of President; neither shall any Person be eligible to that Office who shall not have attained to the Age of thirty five Years, and been fourteen Years a Resident within the United States.

In Case of the Removal of the President from Office, or of his Death, Resignation, or Inability to discharge the Powers and Duties of the said Office, the Same shall devolve on the Vice President, and the Congress may by Law provide for the Case of Removal, Death, Resignation or Inability, both of the President and Vice President, declaring what Officer shall then act as President, and such Officer shall act accordingly, until the Disability be removed, or a President shall be elected.

The President shall, at stated Times, receive for his Services, a Compensation, which shall neither be encreased nor diminished during the Period for which he shall have been elected, and he shall not receive within that Period any other Emolument from the United States, or any of them.

Before he enter on the Execution of his Office, he shall take the following Oath or Affirmation:—"I do solemnly swear (or affirm) that I will faithfully execute the Office of the President of the United States, and will to the best of my Ability, preserve, protect and defend the Constitution of the United States."

Section 2. The President shall be Commander in Chief of the Army and Navy of the United States, and of the Militia of the several States, when called into the actual Service of the United States; he may require the Opinion, in writing, of the principal Officer in each of the executive Departments, upon any Subject relating to the Duties of their respective Offices, and he shall have Power to grant Reprieves and Pardons for Offences against the United States, except in Cases of Impeachment.

He shall have Power, by and with the Advice and Consent of the Senate, to make Treaties, provided two thirds of the Senators present concur; and he shall nominate, and by and with the Advice and Consent of the Senate, shall appoint Ambassadors, other public Ministers and Consuls, Judges of the supreme Court, and all other Officers of the United States, whose Appointments are not herein otherwise provided for, and which shall be established by Law: but the Congress may by Law vest the Appointment of such inferior Officers, as they think proper, in the President alone, in the Courts of Law, or in the Heads of Departments.

The President shall have Power to fill up all Vacancies that may happen during the Recess of the Senate, by granting Commissions which shall expire at the End of their next Session.

Section 3. He shall from time to time give to the Congress Information of the State of the Union, and recommend to their consideration such Measures as he shall judge necessary and expedient; he may, on extraordinary Occasions, convene both Houses, or either of them, and in Case of Disagreement between them, with Respect to the Time of Adjournment, he may adjourn them to such Time as he shall think proper; he shall receive Ambassadors and other public Ministers; he shall take Care that the Laws be faithfully executed, and shall Commission all the Officers of the United States.

Section 4. The President, Vice President and all civil Officers of the United States shall be removed from office on Impeachment for, and Conviction of, Treason, Bribery, or other high Crimes and Misdemeanors.

ARTICLE III

Section 1. The judicial Power of the United States, shall be vested in one supreme Court, and in such inferior Courts as the Congress may from time to time ordain and establish. The Judges, both of the supreme and inferior Courts, shall hold their Offices during good Behaviour, and shall, at stated Times, receive for their Services, a

Compensation which shall not be diminished during their Continuance in Office.

Section 2. The judicial Power shall extend to all Cases, in Law and Equity, arising under this Constitution, the Laws of the United States, and Treaties made, or which shall be made, under their Authority;—to all Cases affecting Ambassadors, other public Ministers and Consuls;—to all Cases of admiralty and maritime Jurisdiction;—to Controversies to which the United States shall be a Party;—to Controversies between two or more States;—between a State and Citizens of another State;—between Citizens of different States;—between Citizens of the same State claiming Lands under Grants of different States, and between a State, or the Citizens thereof, and foreign States, Citizens or Subjects.

In all Cases affecting Ambassadors, other public Ministers and Consuls, and those in which a State shall be a Party, the supreme Court shall have original Jurisdiction. In all the other Cases before mentioned, the supreme Court shall have appellate Jurisdiction, both as to Law and Fact, with such Exceptions, and under such Regulations as the Congress shall make.

The Trial of all Crimes, except in Cases of Impeachment, shall be by Jury; and such Trial shall be held in the State where the said Crimes shall have been committed; but when not committed within any State, the Trial shall be at such Place or Places as the Congress may by Law have directed.

Section 3. Treason against the United States shall consist only in levying War against them, or in adhering to their Enemies, giving them Aid and Comfort. No Person shall be convicted of Treason unless on the Testimony of two Witnesses to the same overt Act, or on Confession in open Court.

The Congress shall have Power to declare the Punishment of Treason, but no Attainder of Treason shall work Corruption of Blood, or Forfeiture except during the Life of the Person attainted.

Section 1. Full Faith and Credit shall be given in each State to the public Acts, Records, and judicial Proceedings of every other State. And the Congress may by general Laws prescribe the Manner in which such Acts, Records, and Proceedings shall be proved, and the Effect thereof.

Section 2. The Citizens of each State shall be entitled to all Privileges and Immunities of Citizens in the several States.

A Person charged in any State with Treason, Felony, or other Crime, who shall flee from Justice, and be found in another State, shall, on Demand of the executive Authority of the State from which he fled, be delivered up, to be removed to the State having Jurisdiction of the Crime.

No Person held to Service or Labour in one State, under the Laws thereof, escaping into another, shall, in Consequence of any Law or Regulation therein, be discharged from such Service or Labour, but shall be delivered up on Claim of the Party to whom such Service or Labour may be due.

Section 3. New States may be admitted by the Congress into this Union; but no new State shall be formed or erected within the Jurisdiction of any other State; nor any State be formed by the Junction of two or more States, or Parts of States, without the Consent of the Legislatures of the States concerned as well as of the Congress.

The Congress shall have Power to dispose of and make all needful Rules and Regulations respecting the Territory or other Property belonging to the United States; and nothing in this Constitution shall be so construed as to Prejudice any Claims of the United States, or of any particular State.

Section 4. The United States shall guarantee to every State in this Union a Republican Form of Government, and shall protect each of them against Invasion; and on Application of the Legislature, or of the

Executive (when the Legislature cannot be convened) against domestic Violence.

ARTICLE V

The Congress, whenever two thirds of both Houses shall deem it necessary, shall propose Amendments to this Constitution, or, on the Application of the Legislatures of two thirds of the several States, shall call a Convention for proposing Amendments, which, in either Case, shall be valid to all Intents and Purposes, as Part of this Constitution, when ratified by the Legislatures of three fourths of the several States, or by Conventions in three fourths thereof, as the one or the other Mode of Ratification may be proposed by the Congress; Provided that no Amendment which may be made prior to the Year One thousand eight hundred and eight shall in any Manner affect the first and fourth Clauses in the Ninth Section of the First Article; and that no State, without its Consent, shall be deprived of its equal Suffrage in the Senate.

ARTICLE VI

All Debts contracted and Engagements entered into, before the Adoption of this Constitution, shall be as valid against the United States under this Constitution, as under the Confederation.

This Constitution, and the Laws of the United States which shall be made in Pursuance thereof; and all Treaties made, or which shall be made, under the Authority of the United States, shall be the supreme Law of the Land; and the Judges in every State shall be bound thereby, any Thing in the Constitution or Laws of any State to the Contrary notwithstanding.

The Senators and Representatives before mentioned, and the Members of the several State Legislatures, and all executive and judicial Officers, both of the United States and of the several States, shall be bound by Oath or Affirmation, to support this Constitution; but no religious Test shall ever be required as a Qualification to any Office or public Trust under the United States.

The Ratification of the Conventions of nine States, shall be sufficient for the Establishment of this Constitution between the States so ratifying the Same.

Done in Convention by the Unanimous Consent of the States present the Seventeenth Day of September in the Year of our Lord one thousand seven hundred and Eighty seven and of the Independence of the United States of America the Twelfth
In witness whereof We have hereunto subscribed our Names.

Attest *William Jackson*
Secretary

Go. Washington—Presidt.
and deputy from Virginia.

NEW HAMPSHIRE *John Langdon*
Nicholas Gilman

MASSACHUSETTS *Nathaniel Gorham*
Rufus King

CONNECTICUT *Wm. Saml. Johnson*
Roger Sherman

NEW YORK *Alexander Hamilton*

NEW JERSEY *Wil: Livingston*
David Brearley.
Wm. Paterson.
Jona: Dayton

PENNSYLVANIA *B Franklin*
Thomas Mifflin
Robt Morris
Geo. Clymer

Thos FitzSimons
Jared Ingersoll
James Wilson
Gouv Morris

DELAWARE *Geo: Read*
Gunning Bedford jun
John Dickinson
Richard Bassett
Jaco: Broom

MARYLAND *James McHenry*
Dan of St Thos Jenifer
Danl Carroll

VIRGINIA *John Blair*
James Madison Jr.

NORTH CAROLINA *Wm. Blount*
Richd. Dobbs Spaight.
Hu Williamson

SOUTH CAROLINA *J. Rutledge*
Charles Cotesworth Pinckney
Charles Pinckney
Pierce Butler.

GEORGIA *William Few*
Abr Baldwin

In Convention Monday, September 17th. 1787.

PRESENT THE STATES OF
New Hampshire, Massachusetts; Connecticut, Mr. Hamilton from

New York, New Jersey, Pennsylvania, Delaware, Maryland, Virginia, North Carolina, South Carolina and Georgia.

Resolved,

That the preceding Constitution be laid before the United States in Congress assembled, and that it is the Opinion of this Convention, that it should afterwards be submitted to a Convention of Delegates, chosen in each State by the People thereof, under the Recommendation of its Legislature, for their Assent and Ratification; and that each Convention assenting to, and ratifying the Same, should give Notice thereof to the United States in Congress assembled.

Resolved,

That it is the Opinion of this Convention, that as soon as the Conventions of nine States shall have ratified this Constitution, the United States in Congress assembled should fix a Day on which Electors should be appointed by the States which shall have ratified the same, and a Day on which the Electors should assemble to vote for the President, and the Time and Place for commencing Proceedings under this Constitution. That after such Publication the Electors should be appointed, and the Senators and Representatives elected: That the Electors should meet on the Day fixed for the Election of the President, and should transmit their votes certified signed, sealed and directed, as the Constitution requires, to the Secretary of the United States in Congress assembled, that the Senators and Representatives should convene at the Time and Place assigned; that the Senators should appoint a President of the Senate, for the sole Purpose of receiving, opening and counting the Votes for President; and, that after he shall be chosen, the Congress, together with the President, should, without Delay, proceed to execute this Constitution.

By the Unanimous Order of the Convention.

W. Jackson Secretary. *Go. Washington* Presidt.